D0762718

Guild Repertoire

piano music appropriate for the auditions of the National Guild of Piano Teachers

Selected and Edited **by Leo Podolsky**
in collaboration with **June Davison** and **Ardella Schaub**

I have long held the idea that an organized curriculum is of great importance in assuring the consistent progress of piano pupils. Therefore, when Dr. Podolosky suggested that he, with his associates June Davison and Ardella Schaub, compile, grade and edit a series of books of repertoire appropriate for the auditions of the National Guild of Piano Teachers, he found me receptive to the idea. The goals and grade classifications of the Guild have always been related to representative types of compositions. While the Guild Syllabus outlines these requirements in general, Dr. Podolsky's project provides specific materials to meet them. Although the GUILD REPERTOIRE is particularly suited to the auditions of the National Guild of Piano Teachers, it furnishes a well-balanced curriculum for piano pupils in general.

IRL ALLISON, *Founder-President*
National Guild of Piano Teachers

Copyright © 1959 Summy-Birchard Music
A division of Summy-Birchard Inc.

All rights reserved.   Printed in U.S.A.
ISBN 0-87487-643-5

Summy-Birchard Inc.
exclusively distributed by
Alfred Publishing Co., Inc.

CONTENTS

INTERMEDIATE C

INTERMEDIATE D

Praeludium

Johann Sebastian Bach
(1685-1750)

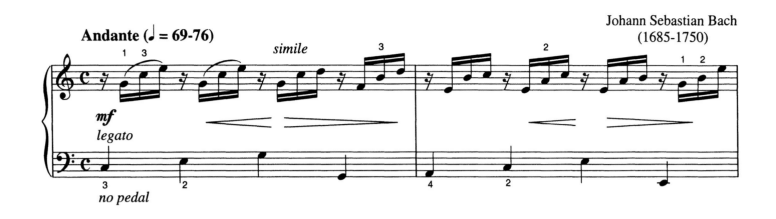

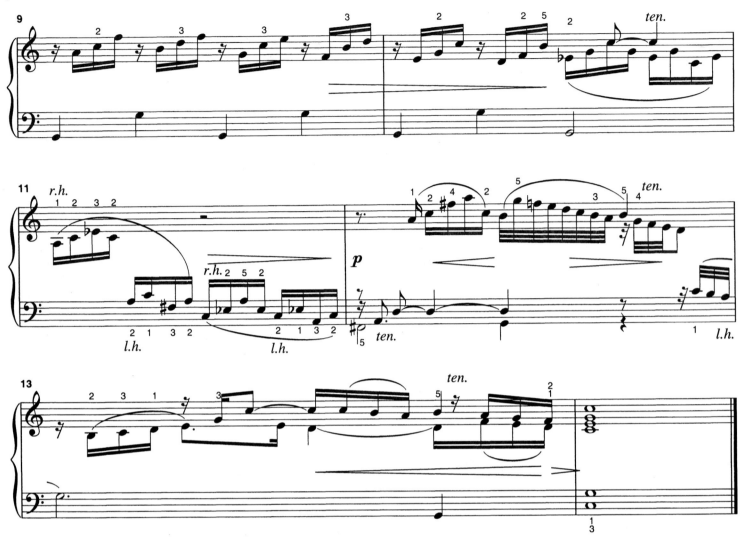

Prelude

Johann Sebastian Bach
(1685-1750)

Moderato (♩ = 96-108)

* Broken chord begins on the beat.

Ländler

Wolfgang Amadeus Mozart
(1756-1791)

Study for Right
or
Left Hand Alone

Carl Philipp Emanuel Bach
(1714-1788)

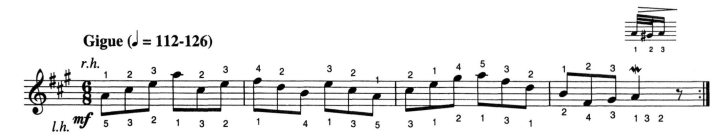

Play left hand one octave lower than written.

Für Elise

Ludwig van Beethoven
(1770-1827)

Poco moto (♪ = 120-132)

Meno mosso (♩ = 100-108)

Sonatina

Muzio Clementi, Op.36, No. 3
(1752-1832)

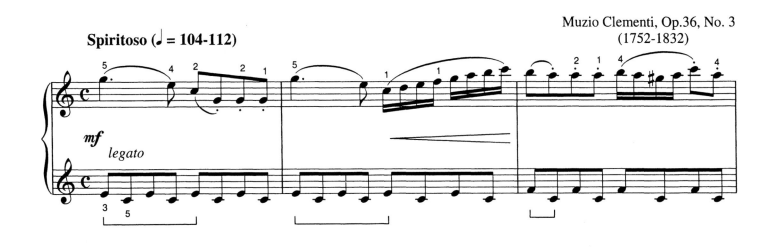

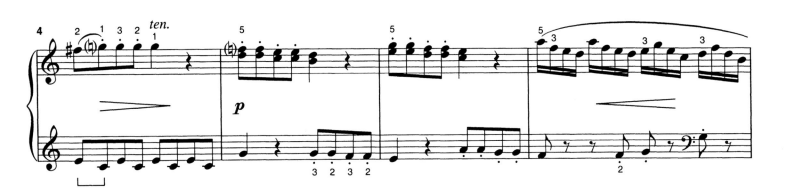

0643

0643

Sonatina

Gustav Merkel, Op. 173, No. 1
(1827-1885)

Allegretto (♩ = 138 - 152)

Avalanche

Stephen Heller, Op. 45, No. 2
(1814-1888)

Russian Folk Dance

Peter I. Tchaikovsky
(1840-1893)

Waltz

Edvard Grieg, Op. 38, No. 7
(1843-1907)

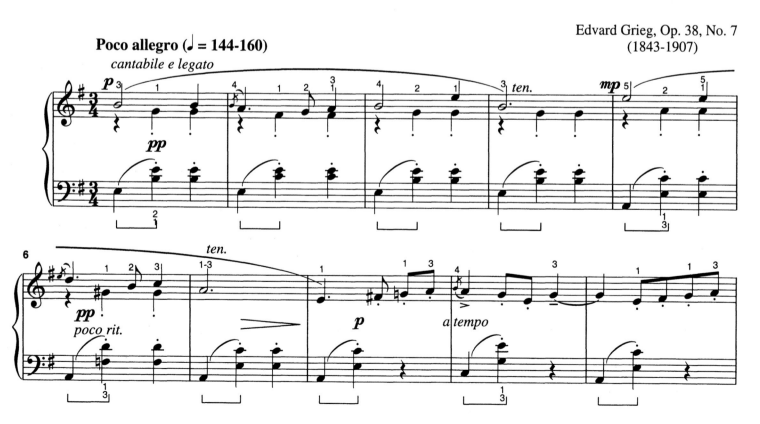

0643

Waltz

Vladimir Rebikov
(1866-1919)

Waltz

S. Zaranek

Lightly, gracefully (♩. = 58-62)

Humorous Etude

B. Gorodinsky

Not too fast (♩ = 112-128)

Praeludium

George Frederic Handel
(1685-1759)

Prelude

Johann Sebastian Bach
(1685-1750)

Moderato (♩ = 108-120)

* The broken chord begins on the beat.

Solfeggietto

Carl Philipp Emanuel Bach
(1714-1788)

Allegro ($\quad$ = 126-144)

Gavotte

Poco allegro (♩ = 84-96)

Stephen Clark

Sonatina

Johann Ladislaus Dussek, Op. 20, No. 1
(1760-1812)

RONDO

Allegretto Tempo di minuetto (♩ = 104-116)

2nd time to Coda

Minore

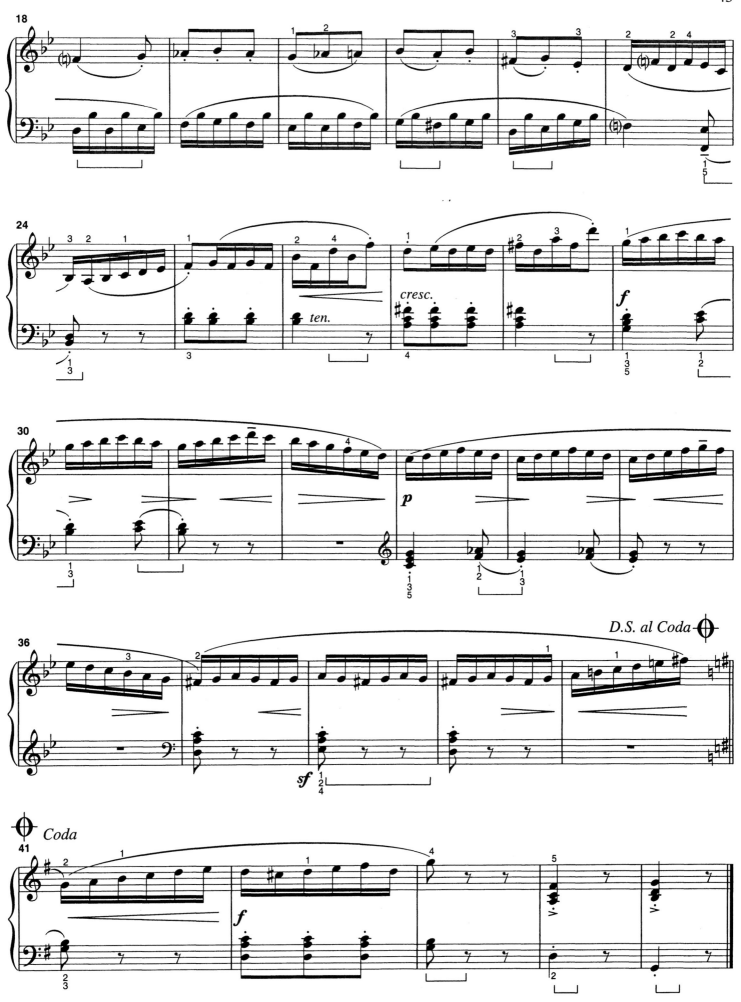

Sonatina

Friedrich Kuhlau, Op. 88, No. 3
(1786-1832)

Allegro burlesco (♩ = 104-112)

Grandmother Tells
a Ghost Story

Theodor Kullak, Op. 81, No. 3
(1818-1882)

Petite Tarantella

Stephen Heller, Op. 46, No. 7
(1814-1888)

Lyric Waltz

Dmitri Shostakovich
(1906-1975)

Con moto (♩ = 160-184)

Dots

S. Wolfenzon

Spring Tune

A. Freed

Con moto (♩ = 126-144)

mf leggiero

The Hungry Cat
and the Well-Fed Cat

Slowly, sorrowfully (♩ = 60-69)

W. Salmanov